He Disturbed Her Soul

A slap, punch, and kick on the road to mental recovery!

Tenika Jimenez

ISBN: 978-0-578-59434-7

Printed in the United States of America

To subscribe to Tenika's book, *He Disturbed Her Soul*, you can sign up at www.mailchimps.com/hedisturbedhersoul. Also, you can follow Tenika and watch videos at www.facebook.com/hedisturbedhersoulbook.

DEDICATION

To my beloved children, Tarel, Ahmante, and Jaekel, who are devoted to their mom. You are blessed and dear to my heart and soul. You all have supported me through everything, even my craziness. Your faith in me has been the cornerstone of my existence. With you all, I have overcome trials and tribulations. Everything that I am today I owe it all to God and you three; I will always love you more and more each day. Thank you for believing in me and pushing me to be better for all of us.

To my cousin, Shylo Rodriguez, whose sole job was being a listening ear when I had no one to talk to. You came through for me time and time again. You have been my rock. On days when I couldn't see what was available to me, you came with the bounceback answers and got me right back on track. For that, I owe it to you to let you know that you have been part of my recovery process. I love you to death. You are my "Holy Ghost Snapback Queen." Thank you for all those long talks and encouraging words.

To my friend and sister in Christ, Renee Love, you have been an inspiration to me since the first day we met. God aligned our spirits together, and we have been friends ever since. You motivated me when I wanted to give up, and you didn't even know you were doing it. You held my hand in spirit and guided me through my recovery process. I love you for each moment you took the time to embrace me. Thank you for your love and support.

ACKNOWLEDGEMENTS

I would like to give special thanks to Pastor Jesse Curney III for providing me with a place to go and worship the Lord. My experience in prayer at New Mercies Christian Church has changed my life forever. I will always have a love for the altar of this house of God.

TABLE OF CONTENTS

INTRODUCTION

My gift was a calling, and I was ready to answer! I was sitting alone at home, and I knew God was calling me to share my story. At this point, I hadn't taken inventory of my life and all the blessings. I couldn't see how my life was going.

In this book, you will read stories about my life and how the lessons I learned taught me to build the posture I walk in now. I was told that I was "no good" and that "no one was going to want me." I was told that I was useless, but look at what my life has become. I made it through the miserable, self-pitying phase of my life. There was nothing else that could have gotten in my way of moving forward and becoming the woman I am today. I had to face trials and tribulations in order to be able to share my stories with the world. No one would have known any of these things about me or could have even imagined I went through any of what I have written in this book.

I don't look like what I have been through. In the past three years I have struggled with depression, anxiety, hurt, pain, suicidal thoughts, and abuse. I realized I had been through a lot. When I relocated and began doing things for myself, living out the dreams and goals I had set for myself, suddenly an overwhelming sense of accomplishment came over me.

The things I had prayed for were all happening; my dreams were coming true. I said I was going to get my GED, and I did it in six months. I said I was going to launch my business, and I did it in one year. I said I was going to write a book to help others, and I did it in a few months. I was focused on making my life better for my children and I.

I wanted my past to be my past. I'm not saying I got over everything that happened; I left my abuser only one year ago. What I'm saying is that getting out of that relationship helped me, so I was able to clear my mind and change a lot of my toxic behavioral patterns.

Domestic abuse did not stop me. It gave me a platform to speak for myself, as well as other men and women who are afraid to say something. My success is not the house I live in, the car I drive, or the clothes I wear. For the most part, it's connected to the money I make and the things I am able to provide for my children and myself. Anyone who knows me well will say that money is not the biggest part of my success. It is being able to help the homeless and give to those who need it more than I do.

Where is your voice? You may have an idea about your voice. You have all the right answers here in these pages. This is the kind of blessed life that I want you to start living. You can become who you want to be. I know that being with and loving someone who is toxic is a hard thing to let go of because you think that this person is right for you. Sometimes you have to step back and take a close look at them to see if what you really want is in them. Ask yourself: Am I happy? Is this the person I want to be with? Hurt people cannot make you happy; they can only hurt you.

People who are unhappy and not living the lives that they want for themselves cannot help you with your dreams and goals. Why? Because they have no idea what they want and will turn your life around when they see that you are striving to become better.

Toxic relationships only lead to destruction. As you continue reading this book, you will learn all about what I went through and how I was able to get away from my toxic relationships. You will also read about how God changed my life in the midst of my storms.

PART ONE:

RELEASING AND LETTING GO

Chapter 1

MINDSET

When I first owned my truth about how I was in so many relationships that didn't turn out the way I thought they would, it all became clear to me that I did not know who I was, what I wanted, what I liked, or how much I was worth. Not having the love of my family is one reason I think that I made so many mistakes in my relationships.

Watching my mother, sister, and aunts, I never knew that I would turn out this way. I always thought that seeing them fight in their relationships was a normal thing. I was a child who didn't know any better because I only saw what was in front of me. Who was I to say if it was right or wrong?

It wasn't until I got older and started dating that I began looking for love in the wrong places. I had a son at the age of fifteen. I thought that his father and I would have stayed together, but that didn't work out. We were too young to get married, and his parents wouldn't allow it.

As I grew into a young woman, my relationships with men were never the greatest. Now that I am older, I reflect back on all of my serious relationships and recognize that they were abusive in some way. I don't remember feeling loved the right way. I was the only one who was in love and giving my all. The men were just giving me twenty percent of what they had. Do I regret some of my relationships? Yes, but I learned lessons from all of them.

At some point in my life, I wanted more from the men I was with, but it just never seemed to happen. *I don't recognize myself in the mirror. I have to take my life back.* These thoughts raced through my mind.

I knew I had lost my identity because I was always changing my hair. I began wearing makeup more often and dressing up trying to get my boyfriend's attention (or just any attention at all). I did not look distasteful or raunchy; I just felt like I needed to step my game up to be a little sexier. That's what I thought was the issue. In there, somewhere, I lost who I was because I was trying to please my boyfriend at the time.

You can take back your life, too. You don't have to be unhappy in a relationship. Only you can decide what is best for you. No one has the right to dictate how you should be treated.

I wanted to be free from all the lies I was living. In my relationships, I believed that we were in love; our lives were exactly how we wanted them to be. But I was the

one being untruthful to myself. My real feelings about what was going on in my life were all a lie to myself and everyone around me.

All my life I hid behind the truth: I don't know what love is. I don't know if I even love myself. I couldn't possibly love myself because I allowed others to treat me badly. *Why did they hit me? Why did I just get punched in the face? Am I the one who brought this on myself?* He would say, "Bitch, Imma kill you."

Did he just call me out my name? I convinced myself he had his own personal issues, so he was cruel and ugly to me.

I remember being home one Saturday night. My husband had gone out to work at a wedding. He got home at about 4:00 am. I didn't have any cigarettes, so I asked him if he had one. He replied, "No, I smoked the last one driving home." After knowing this man for so many years, I knew that he always had a cigarette somewhere, no matter what was going on.

On this particular night, he was high off of something other than liquor. We ended up having a full blown argument just because I asked for a cigarette. He was so drunk that I did not want him to sleep in the room because he smelled like a brewery and snored even louder when he is drunk. I told him to sleep in the living room.

I snatched the blanket off of him and tried kicking him out of the bed. He jumped up, went in the drawer, pulled out a gun, and threatened me to leave him alone. Of course, in the back of my mind I thought, *This crazy motha sucka*. I asked if he was going to shoot me. Then, I told him he would go to jail because the kids were around, and they could hear us arguing loud as hell.

Things did not stop there. He went on to call me names and say hurtful things to me. He had a way of making me feel like I was worthless. I called him a drunk and a cokehead. He went on to say to me, "I would rather be a drunk and a cokehead than dying and needing a kidney." At that very moment, I decided I was sleeping with the enemy; he was no longer someone I respected.

I used to fight and argue back. I threw punches and smacks right back. I never stood there and just let them hit me. I'm 5'4" tall and only weigh about 146 pounds. That is not enough to beat a man. God did not build me to be someone's punching bag. That is not what I thought at that time. I thought I was tough enough to fight back and claimed that I was a big bad wolf.

If he hit me, I was gonna do something to him. *Yeah, come on motha sucka. What you got? Is that all you got? You hit like a girl. You no good son of a bitch.* These were things I used to think and say when he pushed or slapped me. Was this the right thing to do? No. But how else was I supposed to defend myself when they began bullying me?

I know now that fighting fire with fire is not the answer, but I didn't know that back then. I will not tell you that I was perfect through it all because that would be a lie. I sacrificed my life and endangered my children to be with my husband, and he took that for granted.

I never told anyone what I used to go through because I knew they couldn't help me if I was just gonna go back to the relationship. Don't be afraid to tell someone what is going on inside of you, even if you are not ready to leave. The steps to getting out are not just about saying you're going to do it over and over in your head. Even when you do tell someone, make sure that it is the right person.

If you had friends like I did, then you're in trouble. Those people did nothing for me but talk about me and laugh behind my back. Their loyalty was to my husband. I was just someone who was telling my business and giving the people in town something to talk about. There were times when I confided in people thinking they cared and could tell me how to get out of or fix the issues, but they couldn't do anything because the issue was inside the person I was with. Being a narcissist, he thought he did no wrong and blamed everything on me.

I felt like I was never going to get away from him. The forces of evil were everywhere around him and my house. The more I prayed, the stronger he became. It seemed like the life was being sucked out of me. The process I went through to begin to change my thoughts was the most difficult thing I had to do in my life because I was taught differently. My mother brought me up learning how to fight men with words and objects, not kind words and love.

Reflection Exercise

Write down two excuses that you use the most and reflect on them. Below, take the two excuses and replace them with two expectations. After you write them down, recite them to yourself every day. This will mark the new beginning of your journey; no more excuses. Also, write your answers down in a journal and date it.

Just because a person says they love you doesn't mean they really do. There must be some actions that follow those words. What expectations did you create for yourself to help change your life? When you begin to change the way you think, your problems will seem much smaller. What will you change to tell yourself you're being loved the right way?

Chapter 2

EMOTIONAL TIES

I asked myself over and over again what was wrong with me. *Is my situation going to get better? How did I end up here?* My mother never let me be a mother to my son when we lived under the same roof. She and her boyfriend would not even let my son's father see him without giving him a hard time. I cannot explain the whole situation to this day. All I know is that my mother fought me if I disciplined my son. She would take him to my sister's house, and she wouldn't tell me where they were going.

My mother completely excluded me from my own son's life. Instead of her helping me to become a better mother to my son, she took that away from me. Now, I don't have a relationship with him. Emotionally, I am not attached to him. We don't speak at all, and I blame my mother and sister for coming in between us all these years.

My mother was never there for me. When I needed emotional support or any kind of advice, I couldn't go to her because she wasn't much of a parent to me. It was like she hated me. I believe that my life could have been different if I had had the right upbringing.

I was a young mother at the age of fifteen. I dropped out of school, ran the streets, and did whatever I wanted to. Because my mother didn't teach me how to be a mother to my child, I got high smoking weed, snorting cocaine, and drinking. Did I have any positive influences in my life around me to show me a different way? No.

One year, I was raped in a park near my house. I remember it was April 1st, my mother's birthday. My mother went over to her sister's house and left me home alone, so I made plans to go hang out with my friends in my old neighborhood. In order for me to get there, I had to take the train. In my neighborhood in Brooklyn, there were these boys who bothered me all the time. Every time they saw me, they said things to me or threw things at me.

On this particular night, it was about 7:00 pm when I began making my way to the L train station. As I walked up Wilson Avenue, I saw two of the boys from the crew and hoped they hadn't seen me. I had on a red coat with fur on the hood, so I put my hood on to keep them from noticing me. That did not work. The boys followed me into the train station. As I was paying for my tokens, one of them came up behind me and started pulling on my hair. I kept telling them to leave me alone and stop touching me.

I must have made them mad because one of them pulled out a knife and told me to walk. I tried to get away from them and run home, but they both grabbed me and pushed me towards the door to leave the train station. The park was around the corner from the train station, and so they both held my arms to keep me from running away. It was crazy because no one was outside that night.

The boys made me walk up the street to the back of the park. Then, they took turns raping me in a dark corner behind the nearby school. One of them cut my neck and leg with the knife. I struggled as they violated me, so they periodically stopped what they were doing, punched me in my head and face, and told me to shut up and stop resisting.

When they were done, all I remember is passing out on the ground because my legs were weak and gave out from under me. These boys must have gone to a friend's house and told them what just had happened because Raheem, a man I knew from the neighborhood, came and picked me up. When he saw that I was bleeding and my face was bruised, he walked me all the way to my block on Schaefer and Central.

I couldn't make it all the way to my house, so I had Raheem sit me down on the corner where my best friend lived. I told him to go get her and tell her what happened. She came outside, and I just cried on her lap. We didn't know what to do, so she walked me down the block.

When I got in the house, I went straight into the shower with all my clothes and everything on. I had no idea what I was doing. I called my aunt's house, and my cousin answered the phone. I told my cousin to call my mother and tell her to come home immediately because I had been raped. My cousin thought I was playing a joke.

When my mother got home, we called the police. They came and took my statement. They also drove me around in their car to see if I could point the boys out to them. Sure enough, the boys were right on the corner of Schaefer and Wilson.

After the boys were caught, I was even more afraid of them because these guys were bad people from the streets. They always threatened to hurt my family members and I after that. I had to go before a grand jury and tell them what happened. I also had to seek counseling, but I didn't. My mother didn't get me the help I needed when I needed it most.

I went from being raped to being abused by my boyfriends. There was a pattern in my life. Throughout the years, I looked for a way out. Even with being brought up in the church and believing that there is a true living God, my life still played out the way it did. Now I know that I had to go through these things in order to be able to tell my story and help others who may be going through the same things I did.

Reflection Exercise

Top 3 Excuses - Write the excuses you make on the line.

1. _____

_____

2. _____

_____

3. _____

_____

Chapter 3

PAST EXPERIENCES

Travis didn't show any signs of being a jerk or seem like someone who could possibly hurt me, so I entered into a relationship with him. I mean, I was starting to really like him. He was attentive, caring, and as handsome as ever. I was still in my early 20s, so I was still pretty young. Travis was a much older man. I liked older men, so his age did not matter to me. Back then, I had just come out of a 10-year relationship with my first son's father. All I know is that I liked Travis, and he was into me.

The journey began the first day we met. We spent hours on the phone talking and getting to know each other. We talked about everything, but I didn't ask the right questions back then. I was more concerned about his job and the money he made. I did not think about what would happen if something went wrong.

I had been living with my mother when I met Travis. Everything seemed to be going okay. We went out on dates and spent time together doing things couples do. Because he was older than me, he taught me how to be a woman. I learned a lot from him.

One day he had plans to go to a formal event, but I didn't wear heels. We were in my apartment one night (he was spending the night), then he took some books and asked me to put them on top of my head. Of course, I began laughing and asking why he wanted me to do this. Unexpectedly, he pulled out a box with a pair of heels in it and told me to put them on. He said he was going to teach me how to walk, and he did. He was preparing me for what was to come in the future; that's how I saw it. I had no idea that I was going to turn into such a lady after being with him. I not only became a lady; I became a woman.

I was sort of a sexy tomboy. I dreamed about marrying Travis. He was my Prince Charming. He was well put together and had his affairs in order in my eyes. I began falling in love with him. I wish I had not fallen in love with him because, after a while, his ex-girlfriend came back into the picture.

Travis told me his ex was looking for closure. I did not care about her getting in the way because I thought I had it going on. She was just someone that I had to make sure wasn't going to get in my way of getting what I wanted from Travis. I knew that she was back from the service and whatever plans she had before she left were shot out the window when she found out about me. He and I were together, so I was not going to give up on our relationship.

I was young, pretty, and made love to him whenever he wanted. I did things for him whenever he asked or needed me to; I treated him like a king. I bathed him, cooked his meals, and washed his clothes. I acted like a wife even before he proposed. I played my role, but things took a turn. The days became shorter and shorter. Travis and I didn't go out as much anymore.

I cannot tell you where it began going left when I thought it was going right. In my eyes, I had a good thing going. Travis and I didn't live together, so I didn't clock his every move. I believed the things he told me. If he was with other women, I didn't know about until later on. To my knowledge, he was my man and mine only.

At this point, my mother had moved out and left me with the apartment, so I was living on my own at 22 years old. I had to get my life together because I had no choice but to be responsible. I trusted Travis. I loved him. I was down for him and would never have hurt him. I was so in love with Travis that I would have given up my life for his. Soon after we became exclusive, I got pregnant. Travis moved in with me but still kept his own place. I went over there when he was not at my house. I called it a place away from home.

Thinking about him as I write this down just makes me smile. The valuable things Travis taught me really helped me along the way. There were instances where I acted like a spoiled brat because I was still young and dumb. I had jealous tendencies; that was the immaturity in me.

I told Travis I loved him and my actions showed it, too. But he did not feel the same. He began playing mind games and confusing me about the relationship; he stopped treating me right. He began seeing other women behind my back and told me they were his "friends." The phone calls became less frequent. The conversations were not as loving as they had been in the beginning. What was I to do? I was fighting for his love. Nothing was going to stop me from getting Travis to marry me. I was willing to pull out all the stops.

As time went by, I had to leave the apartment. I became homeless because my mother did not put my name on the lease. The building manager wanted me out because I hadn't been paying the rent. I had to find a new place to live, so Travis moved his son and I in with him.

Travis took a chance on me. I thought that he had given up on us, but he hadn't (at that moment). He did what he thought was right. On top of that, I did have his child. I thought him being with us would bring us closer, and it did for a little while. Some days were good and some were not, but that is the case in any relationship.

In my mind, I thought he would want to be with me. He stayed with me at the apartment whenever he wanted to. But at this point, I was his part-time girlfriend. And I allowed it. I didn't care because he was paying the rent and taking care of his son. One day I gave him an ultimatum, thinking that was the way to get him to commit to me. The relationship didn't work, and I was put out of his apartment because my name was not put on the lease.

You can't fathom the thoughts I had. Who would believe that this could happen to me twice? First with my mother, and now with Travis. Not me! I was back to square one with nowhere to go. The relationship I had been fighting for was shot to hell.

My friends helped me here and there when they could, so I stayed with them once in a while. That got old quick because they had their own lives and children to deal with. Why would they want to live with my baggage as well? My mother didn't allow me to live with her, even though she had an extra room in her house. She never helped me. My sister had her own place, but she never extended the olive branch to ask me if I needed a place to stay. My life was slowly going downhill, so I decided to leave New York. My brother, who was living in Texas at the time with his wife and kids, let me stay with them.

My relationship with Travis was not a physical one, but it was a mental and emotional one because I loved him dearly with everything I had. I would have done anything for him. I tried to be the perfect girlfriend to him just so that he would commit to me and maybe one day marry me.

Our relationship became rocky. He must have decided that I was not his only option, so he started seeing other women. He began disappearing and not coming home. He gave excuses that he had things to do, then he would wind up staying at his mother's house in Queens.

This pattern continued until Travis stopped coming around and answering my phone calls. I was confused about our relationship. I felt like he didn't want to be with me anymore, and he eventually just stopped coming around. He didn't even stop by to see his son. I guess he had to figure things out. In the meantime, he left me wondering what had happened.

We ended the relationship on his terms. He no longer wanted to be with me. I started to catch him cheating on me, so that triggered me to want to argue and fight all the time. I was jealous because I was young and in love, but I didn't know how to let go. I did not recognize the signs of unreasonable jealousy, domination, control, and humiliation.

You may see this in your own life or relationship. Maybe you're asking yourself how you missed all the various signs of psychological abuse. I had been through so much in my life that I ignored his behavior because I had been grieving the loss of a significant person in my life and wanted to ease my pain somehow.

I jumped into a relationship I had no business being in. Like I said at the beginning of the book, I was young, dumb, and had not changed my thinking until I got older. The wisdom of knowing what real love is didn't come until later on in my life.

At that point, those were the issues in my life and how I dealt with them. I wish that my life had been different. I can't say that I don't regret some of my choices because I do. If I had known that I was going to be mistreated, I would not have gotten involved with any of those men. But no one ever knows where they are starting out in life. When life throws you a curveball, you either hit or miss. In my case, I just kept missing over and over again.

I felt as though I did what any mother would have done to get off the streets when she had no other alternative or family to help her. I couldn't stay with my brother in Texas anymore because he and his wife constantly argued. He did heavy drugs and sold them, too. That put me and my son in danger, so we packed up and went back to New York.

I had been moving from place to place with my son when I met Brian through a friend. He was handsome, sexy, and put it down over the phone. He was charming, sensitive, and talked to me just the way I liked. He came over to my friend's house with his brother, and we hit it off from the first night we met in person. I can't tell you that I wasn't moving quickly or that I had my life together because I didn't. I questioned myself a lot back then. I wasn't sure what was ahead of me when I began dating Brian. He did not show any signs of being abusive, jealous, controlling, or even crazy.

My son and I had been living with my friend for a while until I had to move to a shelter. I called Safe Horizon, explained what happened in my previous relationship, and was allowed to live in the domestic violence shelter. My relationship with Travis never became a severe case of physical abuse, but enough happened to know that I needed help. My son and I lived in the shelter for two years. We had our own room. It was safe, warm, and I didn't have to worry about being asked to leave because some man was coming over. I didn't feel like I wasn't wanted at the shelter.

Travis had no idea where I was for a period of time. It was like I had just disappeared with nowhere to be found. When I returned to New York, he sometimes called my phone and left messages because I didn't answer. I did not want to speak with him because, in my head, he was the reason I was in the shelter. Things would not have turned out like this if he had been sure about himself and the things he wanted in life. But he couldn't provide me with any assurances, so that left me out on the streets to take care of my son alone.

Living in the shelter taught me a few things. I learned structure, stability, and the importance of being responsible for my actions. These were the things that mattered the most. It took me a long time to realize the lessons I was learning at the shelter while I was there. It may not be an easy road for you, but believe in yourself and stand for what you believe in; that's what I did.

I didn't know it at the time, but setting my heart on being with Brian led me right back down another abusive road. When you're not living right or righteously, your life just continues to spin around and around in a circle. It's like the circle constantly reloading until you get it right. I was about to start a new relationship with another man, but I hadn't not fully healed from my previous relationships. I jumped into it with everything I had again.

Brian and I kept in contact even when I went to Texas. We began dating when I moved back to New York, but he wasn't allowed to know where I lived. When I was able to leave the shelter, we met up at different places and spent time together. When it was time for me to go back to the shelter, because I had a curfew, we went our separate ways. Brian and I were together for two years. This was up until I was moved to the second tier, which was the transition stage, to be placed in my own apartment.

My social worker, Maria, called me down often to have weekly meetings and make sure I was ready to leave. She also talked to me about my mental state and advised me to not get mixed up in another abusive relationship. I wish I had listened to her and applied what she told me. You would have thought that I would have listened to her, but I didn't.

While I lived in the shelter, I did everything I was asked to do because a staff member could have called me to say I was approved for an apartment at any time. Finally, I was called about my place. Shortly after finding out about getting approved to move into my apartment, I told Brian that I would be leaving the shelter. Then, I noticed that he began acting strange towards me.

I don't know what happened, but Brian began to treat me differently. He was aggressive with me, and our disagreements turned it screaming matches whenever we were together. I just didn't understand why. I cried and begged him to talk to me. He was so mean to me, but my feelings for him made me vulnerable.

I always thought that I could fix the problem if I just continued to love him. I ignored all the red flags. And I don't know why. Maybe it was because I wanted to make our lives better. We had plans to live together after I got out of the shelter.

One time, I was able to get a pass for the new year, so I made plans to spend time with my friends. I knew that I was going to have a good time with them. I guess Brian was upset because I didn't spend the time with him, but I had explained this to him before I made the plans. He had plans to spend New Year's Day with his family because it was a family tradition, so we both decided that it was ok to be apart. We were going to meet up afterwards.

Apparently, I was so intoxicated and having such a good time that I forgot to call Brian that night. I did not know that he was going to be upset. Anyhow, I finally called him at about four or five o'clock in the morning and asked if I could stop by his house. He said I could, so I bundled up my son (who was three years old at the time) and got in a cab. January in New York usually means snow is falling, so we had to be warm.

When I reached Brian's house and went inside, he seemed fine. It was early in the morning, so we went to his room in his mother's basement. We settled down to go to sleep, and I put my son down. He fell asleep quickly because he was already sleeping when we were in the cab on the way to Brian's house.

Brian and I stayed up for a little while talking, holding each other, and kissing. Everything seemed to be ok, at least that is what I thought while we were getting ready to go to bed. He did not give me any inclination that something was bothering him or that he was upset with me about anything. Brian was a very quiet person quiet when it came to his feelings. You wouldn't know something was wrong until he lashed out at you.

The next day, I had to go back to the shelter because I only had a pass for the night of New Year's Eve. If I didn't return, I would be kicked out of the program. I cannot tell you what triggered Brian, if it was something I said or what he had thought of on his own, but he started an argument with me. He asked me who I was with. He said he had smelled my panties, and they smelled like I had had sex. I mean, he said all kinds of things about how he knew I was with someone else because I got to his house so late.

I knew at that point that I had to get out of his mother's house, but he wouldn't let me leave. He threatened to hurt me if I moved or even said the wrong thing. I had my son with me, so I was scared. I didn't know what Brian was going to do. He went and got a knife from upstairs. Then, he put my son in a room and told him to stay there because he and I were talking. I kept asking Brian to let me leave. He had me pinned down on the floor and began choking me hard. He was strong, so I couldn't fight him. I was scared that I was going to die that day.

My son came out of the room, kneeled down next to me, and asked if I was ok. Brian was still on top of me at this point. I think he lost his mind because he punched me repeatedly in the face. I was weak from him twisting my arm and holding me down on the ground. He was so strong that I couldn't get away.

I thought I was going to lose my life that day. It was already going on two o'clock in the morning, so I had missed my curfew. I kept asking him to let me go home. *Please don't do this in front of my son!* I begged him to let me hold my son's hand. I bled and felt my swollen face. He just kept saying things that sounded so crazy. It was like he blacked out on me and was in this rage of emotions. I remember asking why he was hurting me. *I didn't do anything, I promise. I didn't cheat on you. I wasn't with anyone else. I love you. I want to be with you. There is no one else.* I had to talk him out of the rage he was in. He was a different person. I saw it in his eyes.

Brian finally got off of me. By this time, I was all beaten up. I had to cover my face with my scarf and pretend that it was freezing outside when I got to the shelter. I had to be buzzed in because it was still a holiday, so the only staff members that were there were security guards. I had to sign in at 2:40 am. I knew I was going to get called to the office after the holiday when the staff checked the time I returned to the shelter.

After I signed in, I went upstairs to my apartment. At a domestic violence shelter, you get a room that looks like an apartment to prepare you for the real thing. There's a bedroom, kitchen, living room, and phone in the space. I was in so much pain that I undressed my son, put on his pajamas, and placed him in the bed. I went in the bathroom to look at my face and began crying because it looked like someone had distorted my face. I thought I needed face reconstruction. I had no idea how I was going to hide this from the staff or my social worker.

Maria called me to her office on Monday morning after the holiday break. When I heard the phone ring, I knew what it was about. I was so scared to go downstairs because my face was still swollen and there were bruises around my lips. I did not want anyone to see me. I lived in a domestic violence shelter, so there was no way around someone not seeing me. I went next door to my neighbor, GiGi, and asked her to help me conceal my face with makeup.

The makeup worked because Maria didn't notice that I was beaten up badly. I did tell her that I was seeing a guy and that he and I had gotten into a fight. I told her that he scared me, but that is all because she wanted to know why I came back so late when knew I had a curfew. Maria went on to lecture me, but all I could think about was how crazy Brian was. I was scared because I had told him where the shelter was when we started dating. I should not have done that, but I trusted him.

I thanked God that the security guard did not see my face as I walked inside the shelter on New Year's Day because I held my son up to cover my bruises. If the guard had seen me, they would have called the authorities that night and woken some people up to come in and address the issue.

That was not the end of it, though. I was so scared of Brian that I stayed away from him for weeks. I didn't take his calls, so he popped up at the shelter and stood across the street waiting for me to go outside. I never left the building. I sent my friend to the store for me. Finally, Brian threatened to ring the bell and ask for me. No one was supposed to know where I stayed, so I had to talk to him to keep him from getting me kicked out. I couldn't risk losing my place, so I agreed to meet him at the park near the shelter. That was the day I wrote my own eulogy.

Brian began the conversation with the typical apology. *I'm sorry i will never do that to you again. I don't know what made me snap on you like that. I felt like you were lying to me. I promise I will never hurt you again.* Me, being who I was, believed him. He said that he loved my son and I. He wanted to be there for us, so I told him that I forgave him.

I knew deep down I was afraid of Brian. If I didn't tell him what he wanted to hear, he would tell the shelter staff I had broken the rules. I could not risk being kicked out when I was so close to getting my apartment because my son and I were homeless. We had bounced around from place to place, staying with friends. My family would not take us in, so I had to do what I could to survive. In my mind, staying in a relationship with Brian was the best option. I had been through so much in my life that my judgement was cloudy.

Move-in day finally came. After two years at the domestic violence shelter, I got my own place. I was given a one-bedroom apartment in Bland Houses, which was in the projects in Flushing, Queens. I didn't care what the apartment looked like. It was mine! The feeling I felt when I turned the key in the door brought a sigh of relief. I cried tears of joy on some days when I sat in the living room listening to music or cleaning the house. I made my apartment a home for my son and I.

I had a lot to be proud of because living in a domestic violence shelter wasn't easy. There were nights when I wanted to give up. There were days when I felt hopeless. *Was my situation ever going to change?* I asked myself over and over again if something was wrong with me. *How did I end up here?*

I took Brian back, and he moved in with me. In the beginning, everything was peaches and cream. We were loving and couldn't keep our hands off of each other. Then, he began to change. He became more frustrated with me, and we argued more. I didn't know what a narcissist looked like. I didn't even think that he would behave in an abusive way again after what we had already been through. It was silly to think he was going to change.

I became more demanding of him to get a job, and he felt as though he wasn't appreciated for the things he did do around the house like cooking and cleaning. I did appreciate him, but I saw no reason why I had to fund him when he wanted to hang out with friends.

I was stupid for being with him after he hurt me the first time. I was insecure and attracted abusive men. I went back to him and did whatever he wanted me to do. Do I have an explanation as to why? No. If you asked me why I went back, I might just say it was because I did not know any better. I thought that was love.

When you think you're in love and have never really felt what true love is, you will believe that you can make it work with what you have or what you have been shown all your life. I constantly asked myself what true love looked like. *Was it being beat on? Was it being yelled at or cursed out? Was true love being cheated on and told that you would never be hurt again? Was believing in someone more than you believe in yourself true love?* Ask yourself these questions and reflect on your answers.

My version of love was being with toxic men who cheated on me, beat me, used me, and talked to me disrespectfully. I didn't respect them either, though. Respect is something people have to earn; it is not freely given. If you are in a relationship with someone you don't trust or respect, ask yourself and that person why you two are together. These are things I did not know when I was younger, but I know them now. It's easier for me to recognize patterns before I get into another relationship with someone who may possibly be toxic.

When you're running from someone or something that is hurting you, you become emotionally unstable. If our emotions don't align with what is going on in our lives, our focus will be unstable as well. *Why? When? How? Why do we stay? When do we leave? How come we still love the ones who hurt us?* We wonder how he or she could say they love us when they say horrible things to us. The words cut to the core of our hearts.

I stayed in my relationships because I had very low self-esteem and didn't have anyone to talk to. The people in my life did not talk to me about how to deal with my emotions. I grew up in a household where I watched my mother get beaten up by her men. Sometimes my brother and I jumped in the middle of her fights. We defended my mother without even knowing that we were being affected by the situation. The fights that went on in my house between my mother and the men in her life were so intense that the cops were called to our house.

Ever since I was a little girl, I can remember my mother was always being abused by her husband or boyfriends. All I know is that watching my mother go from one relationship to another with different men didn't teach me anything. I thought that was a normal thing to do. Perhaps that is why I now have four children by four different men, just like my mother. They say life is a cycle, and you go through some of the same things your parents did because they are the ones who raised you.

Our subconscious remembers the physical and verbal abuse, but our conscious mind doesn't remember anything about it. As children, we don't understand what is going on between adults. We don't recognize problems because a few days or weeks go by and everything seems to be normal again. We tend to forget that just a while ago the person we love, who claimed to love us, just beat us up. They said some really harsh things or cursed us out, but we hid it away because we chose to ignore it. When we don't acknowledge the signs, we think we are still in love. We're having sex or back in the kitchen cooking a meal like nothing ever happened. Our thoughts of the abuse are always there in the back of our minds, but we mask them with excuses.

Once we have suffered abuse in our homes growing up or even watched it happen, we adapt to it. I think that is what happened with me because that is what I attracted: abuse. I was abused by my brother, something I never talked about until after he passed away.

My brother used to touch me when my mother left us alone at home. One night, we were staying over my sister's father's house and were sleeping on the floor. Of course, my mother was out partying. I was maybe four or six years old. I didn't know that my brother putting his fingers in my vagina and kissing me was wrong. Even when I got older, I thought that being that close meant we loved each other the most. Now that I think about it, that behavior was sickening.

I didn't have anyone stable in my life to tell me what my brother was doing was wrong. On top of that, I never said anything to anyone until after he passed away. The day after his funeral, my sister and I went over to my aunt's house for dinner with my cousin. We stood outside my aunt's house talking about the funeral and my brother's life. I told them how my brother used to touch me when I was younger. The look on their faces was priceless. I don't think they were ready for me to reveal such a thing; they couldn't believe what I had just said about my brother. I felt relieved once I said it because I had been holding on to that in my mind and heart for years.

Whether they believed me or not, I knew what I said was true. I forgave my brother because I did not know it was wrong back then. I was a little girl, and he was my brother. I went on with my life and never mentioned it again. I don't know if they ever told my mother. If she does know, there is not much she can do about it now because he is no longer with us. I just hope and pray that he was set free.

It took me years to realize I had been broken since I was a child and didn't even know it. *How could I have made these abusive relationships any different?* The answer is that I couldn't. I wasn't the only one damaged--my partners were, too. If you're with someone who is abusive, pay close attention to that person and his or her mood swings.

Reflection Exercise

Top 3 expectations - Write your expectations for your relationships on the line.

1. _____

_____

2. _____

_____

3. _____

_____

Chapter 4

INSECURITIES

I was vulnerable, weak, and insecure. I used to write in my journal how ugly I thought I was because I didn't feel sexy. I didn't feel as though I lived up to who others wanted me to be. I had low self-esteem because of my looks. I knew I was a beautiful person because I got compliments from a lot of people, but I didn't get them from the man I was with at the time. Because of this, I suffered from feelings of insecurity. I believed that no one was going to want me because I already had four children by four different men.

After I became sick, I was done with relationships and finding real love. *Who is gonna love me and want to take care of me? I am now a burden on someone else.* These were some of the thoughts I had because of the way I was treated in my toxic marriage. I couldn't see anything else. My mind was consumed with toxic behavior, and I was filled with hatred. My heart was black. Even though I was in a relationship and tried to make it work, things just seemed to always fail. On days when I thought things were going right, they really weren't.

I hoped to one day love again and leave my past behind, but it wasn't easy. I didn't believe anyone, so I had to learn how to trust again. Building trust with someone you hardly know, but thought you did for many years, is complicated when that person is a narcissist. If there is no trust between two people, there is no relationship. When the narcissist knows you've figured it out, he or she will begin to use guilt, fear, and obligation to draw you back into his or her cycle. If the narcissist sees that none of those strategies work, he or she will try to make you feel as if he or she doesn't want you.

I felt robbed of love in all of my relationships. The physical, mental, and verbal abuse was too much. There was so much strife in these men's lives that I felt my life was no better than theirs with every slap, punch, and kick they gave me. At that time, it really wasn't. I was just like those men who hurt me. I wanted to hurt them, too.

I became ugly inside and out. I wanted to make the men I was with feel the same hurt and pain I felt each time I didn't get what I wanted or needed from them. After all the years of abuse and damage that took place in my life, why couldn't I treat them the same way they treated me? Hell, if it was good enough for them, then it was good enough for me.

My mindset shifted. If "my man" began cheating on me, I was going to turn around and cheat on him. If he called me names and disrespect me, I did the same thing back to him. I went along with his stupidity and childish ways.

For my 40th birthday, I planned to have a huge party at my bar and grill. Everyone was expected to dress up in their best formal wear. I wore a beautiful black princess gown and felt so special. The party was epic, until the end of the night when my husband picked a fight with me. He ended up punching me in the face and ruined everything because he was drunk or under the influence of drugs.

Mental and emotional abuse is debilitating, so you really have to watch out for the signs and make sure to love yourself first. I loved everyone else but myself. I wanted to please other people and make sure they liked me by doing things for them; I didn't think about myself.

When I needed help, no one was around. There were days when I couldn't even get up and cook. My husband left me in the house for hours at a time. Even if I called and asked him to bring me something to eat, it would be hours before he returned with food. Apparently, whatever he had to do was more important than taking care of me.

After a while, I stopped caring about anyone or anything because my house was crumbling to pieces. I was withering away slowly. I began taking out all of the anger I felt towards my husband out on my children. I yelled, screamed, cursed, and hit them for no reason; my temper was through the roof.

I couldn't control my actions or feelings because of this man. I had done so much for him, so I didn't understand why he didn't treat me well. Even before all the infidelity took place, he wasn't good to me. On our wedding night, he had a look on his face like he had just made a mistake. He even went as far as to say, "I think I should have waited." I couldn't believe it.

My husband must have been really shaken after we exchanged our vows because we didn't consummate our marriage until two weeks after the wedding. I suspect he only did that because I called one of his closest friends to tell him that my husband was acting funny. He was so drunk the night we got married that we drove separate cars and didn't go on our honeymoon. We went straight to the club after our wedding reception. I went to the club with my wedding dress on. How tacky is that?

I did so many things to show that I loved this man. All he did was bring strife and transgression into our home. I was so blinded by his actions that I couldn't see that he was using me. If he told the story about our marriage, he would probably say that I messed everything up because I didn't believe in or support him. This was just another one of his narcissistic traits; he loved making people think he was such a good husband to me.

Behind closed doors, no one knew the agony that man put me through. The words he said to me cut me like a sword each time. This man went even so far as to tell our son that he wasn't his real father. After that, I went into such a depression that nothing he ever said to me hurt. It's like a wall went up and everything he threw at me was blocked. I began completely ignoring him as if he didn't exist. The hatred I had for him was so strong that I let it consume me. My health was deteriorating, just like my relationship.

I had no one to turn to and nowhere to go. I talked to my nurses at dialysis, and it felt like they were listening. However, it didn't change the fact that I was living with someone who had become my enemy. I no longer saw my husband as someone I could love or respect as a human being because he didn't respect me, my health, or my life. I didn't care about his needs in our marriage. If the shoe had been on the other foot, I would have never done him wrong.

I have released my husband of all his wrongdoings and forgiven him of his infidelities. At one point, I remember feeling like I was in a whirlwind of doubt and confusion. I asked myself a series of questions: *Are you living or just existing in this man's life? Does he really love you like he says he does?*

Letting go and releasing someone who has hurt you in multiple ways is not for them; it is for you. It helps you move on with your life to grow into a better person for you, your children, and those around you. After I released my ex, I began to make my life the number one priority. This helped me break out of his cycle of abuse. I no longer felt like I was fighting for attention, love, or romance.

There was a pattern in all my relationships, but I didn't notice it until I sat down and thought about every man I had been with. I needed a way to heal from all the damage that had been done to me over the years. If I didn't reflect on my past, I could not have gotten over my insecurities or looked toward my future. I learned a lot from my past and was able to move forward to do the best I could with the cards I was dealt. You can do the same. Just use what you have learned from your healing process.

PART TWO:

RELEASING AND LETTING GO

Chapter 5

POOR PARENTING

My own mother turned her back on me, and I will probably never know why she just gave up on me. It's like she wanted me around to beat up on me. When she took custody of my firstborn, it was like a slap in the face. She didn't trust me with my own child. She wouldn't let me raise my son, not even as I got older. I needed my mother to be there for me when I had no one. She wasn't there to support me, give me advice about how I should do things, or even help me figure out how to make my marriage work.

I believe that my mother took my son and mistreated me because she needed to feel loved. She knew that my son was going to love and cherish her. I love my mom, but I love her from a distance because a lot of my emotional abuse came from her. She kicked me out her house when I went to visit her. When I was homeless, she didn't offer to take my son and I in. We lived in different places, even at strangers' houses. I rented a room in a man's basement one winter because my son and I had nowhere to go.

When life got really tough while I was in Texas with my brother and his family, I wanted her to tell me to return to New York because she would help me. She never made that kind of offer. My mother never hugged me or told me she loved me for a long time. I remember calling her to ask if she could stay with me because I was having surgery and needed her help. She agreed, but I never heard anything back from her about it. When I called her house, I found out she had gone to Florida with my sister. She visited my home only once during that time, and she made excuses about why she couldn't visit me.

My mother couldn't interfere with my second baby, though, because she knew Travis wouldn't put up with her nonsense. My mother used the fact that my first son's dad and family didn't care too much for me or their grandchild. She concocted a lie that I had abused my son, even though it wasn't true. My son was not being abused; he was being disciplined with structure. Since my mother didn't know anything about discipline, structure, or stability in her life, she wasn't able to provide for her children.

There are a lot of things I will never know about my mother and why she treated me and her other grandchildren the way she did. I don't think I care to know anymore. For a long time it bothered me, so I questioned myself as a parent. I know I have done some things in my life as a parent that I wish I hadn't, but they were all learning experiences for me.

Looking back at the things I said and did while I was in stressful situations, those were my reactions to the actions I had been shown throughout my life. If I had been shown better, I would have done better. Ask yourself: Do you want to be treated like I was? Probably not. Children do not deserve to be mistreated because of their parents' actions.

Through all of the years my mother mistreated me, I still somehow reached out looking for love and support from her. I never got it. She talked to me, but it wasn't genuine. As she got older, it seemed as if things got worse. She isn't close to my other children, either. Today, she and I don't even speak. I have asked for forgiveness, but I have yet to receive it.

Before, I had to pay my mother to watch her own grandchildren when we went to visit her; my brother and sister never had to. I was never jealous of them because they received more of my mother's attention. It did cause a rift between us, so I just pulled away from them.

I always swore I wasn't going to treat my kids like my mother treated me. Guess what? I did more damage than my mother did because, through all my mess, I didn't pay attention to the things I said to my boys. I was so hurt in my life all the time that I dumped on my children. Whenever my man and I fought, my attitude changed. I'd become enraged. Not realizing it, I took things out on my children. And they didn't understand why. I didn't understand why.

I didn't realize what I was doing until years later when my boys got older. They began to hear the fights, listen to what was being said, and watch me get beaten up. They began to ignore it and say things to me about not taking my anger out on them because my man didn't want to help.

Did I listen to them? Nope. All the anger and frustration I had built up inside didn't allow me to hear or see what I was doing as a parent to my children. All I could hear and see was that I was bitter, angry, and wanted to get rid of my toxic husband who was living in my house.

I saw myself acting like my mother in my home; I said I would never behave that way. The more I acted like my mother, the more I hurt my children. I did not realize how much damage I did because I hadn't owned the fact that I was hurt and broken inside. Hurt people hurt people. I was depressed, filled with anger, bitterness, frustration, other emotions. Because my sons were the closest to me, I took my pain out on them. I regret every bit of those dark periods.

My life as a young mother did not come with instructions. Since my mother wasn't part of my life to help me figure things out, I did the best I could to raise my sons. I had three more sons after my first child, and I did a darn good job raising them. We may have had some bumps along the way, but we made it out together. My children know that I love them with all my heart, and I would never intentionally hurt them. I support my children in everything they want to do in their lives. I would go to the moon and back for them. It wasn't until my sons saw me become sick that my health became more important to them.

Something needed to change. Life was no longer about me. My children and their well-being became the goal. I had to get my husband out of our lives because the house was in turmoil. The kids were fighting with each other, and I was fighting with the children. All of this was going on while this man came and went like nothing was happening in the house.

The whole house was upside down because there was no order or communication between any of us. The kids did not want to be around me, and they stopped wanting to go anywhere with me because they said I was embarrassing. If I asked one of them to make me something to eat and it wasn't done the way I would have done it, I would curse them out.

I knew that tragedy was going to strike if I didn't get out of that house with my children. I am thankful God has taken me out of that dark place and helped me see how I was hurting my babies. If I stayed in that situation and kept treating them that way, I would have given up and lost everything.

It took me stopping to consider my children to learn the most important lesson from it all: my children mirror what they see me doing. I am their first teacher. If I was not a good role model to them, they would have a hard life trying to figure things out on their own. There were plenty of nights when I stayed up crying because I knew I hurt my boys. I didn't want them to hate me because I was weak and couldn't figure out how to get out of the mess I got myself into. My son told me one day, "You chose to marry him not us. Why should we have to be in the middle of your arguments?" That gave me a big reality check.

I'm also grateful to a friend who helped me put things into perspective. She told me one day, "Tenika, don't yell and curse at the boys any more because you're cursing at yourself. Those boys are you." I was so caught up in my mess that I was sending my boys the wrong message. I had to get my act together. I was losing my family slowly but surely because of the abuse I was carrying around with me every day.

I didn't know how to get over what I was going through until I began listening to myself as I spoke to my children, and they began pulling away from me. No one wanted to be around me. My feelings were hurt. I had to change the dynamics of what was transpiring in my home, and that change had to start with me.

In order for you to be a better parent, you have to be a better person. That starts within you. Always communicate. I took it one day at a time. I didn't have the love I needed from my family, so I made a lot of mistakes with my own kids. My mistakes came from not paying attention to what I was doing around my children. I was so caught up chasing behind a man who was using me for whatever he could get from me because he was narcissistic. He thought I was his property and belonged to him for the rest of his life. That was not the case.

Growing up, I watched the women in my family get abused by the men they were with. I can honestly say that all of my family members are somehow dysfunctional. I know that it has to do with their generation and how they were raised. I had to learn how to separate my feelings about my family because I could not treat my children the way my mother treated me. I knew that I had to be a better mom; that is when my journey began. Life took a turn for the better, and I slowly gained my children back. I saw the change in them, as well. There is always room for improvement, if you're willing to do the work.

Chapter 6

DEPRESSION

I met my husband on February 28, 2004 at a club in the City. We were friends before we started dating. My husband was a DJ for rap artists, so he often visited me when he was touring. When he wasn't on the road, I paid for his flights to New York. Soon after, in April, I started flying to Myrtle Beach, South Carolina to see him.

The relationship was new, but I just knew that I was his bad Puertorican girlfriend. I flew out and stayed in a hotel when I went to see him. I thought I was special, but the only reason he did that was because I was spending money on him. I didn't see any of the red flags because he showed me lots of interest. I thought I could keep his attention only on me. Little did I know I was competing with a world full of women he claimed wanted him.

The beginning of our relationship was okay. We laughed, had fun, and did everything together. Originally, I had decided that it was time for me to leave New York, so I planned to move to Florida with my sister and buy a house. But after he and I started becoming more serious, I decided to buy a house in South Carolina instead. I wanted to be near my sister, but I was in love. My husband even offered me some land that belonged to his family.

I left my apartment in Queens but still paid the rent for a few years so that I could have a place to stay when I went back to New York. I remember we went on a trip to Las Vegas because he had a job out there at the House of Blues. I bought the plane tickets and paid for the room. He was passionate, loving, and caring in a noticeable way when I did things like that for him.

The trip ended after we had a physical altercation because of his jealousy. A rap artist, who was a friend, had been calling me while we were in Las Vegas. My friend, who now rests in peace, was performing at the House of Blues that same time. When my husband and I got back to the hotel, we argued, yelled, and called each other names. Then, he punched me in the face, so I hit him back. All I remember is struggling with him around the room. He grabbed me and shoved me in the bathroom. He took my head and shoved it in the toilet bowl.

Before that fight, he had never put his hands on me. After that, it was easy for him to do it again. I should have walked away then. I stayed with him because I loved him, or at least that's what I thought.

I had already bought the house; we had plans to become famous together. He promised he was going to help me with my poetry career. I bought him a $10,000 studio with all kinds of electronic equipment so that we could work together, but he never once acknowledged that I was trying to build a life for us that was productive. He used that studio for himself and his career. He recorded with other people and made commercials and CDs for other people. My life and what I wanted withered away just like I did. He made so many promises but not one of them did he keep.

I was left to wonder why he didn't come home at night. He always claimed he was working in the studio down the road near his dad's house. The kids and I were home alone on plenty of nights. Other nights, I walked down to the studio to spend time with him, but he made me feel like I wasn't wanted. He had his reasons - he was being unfaithful. I dealt with that for years.

I was so blind. I was in another state without friends or family. He didn't want me to go with him to the clubs when he had to work because he thought I would prevent women from approaching him. He didn't want anyone to know he was in a relationship. I was a secret.

We fought so many times because of his infidelity. I went through his phone and found stains on his clothes. It was so bad that we got into physical fights and the cops had to be called to the house. I felt trapped inside my mind, body, and soul. I was lost in that house, yet I still stayed year after year. I tried working on our marriage. I prayed that God would fix it. I stayed in the relationship for more than 10 years; I endured 17 years of abuse.

One night, I decided to start going out to the clubs by myself and showing up to the places where he DJ'd. I had to see why he didn't want me around. It was obvious that he was cheating. He was famous because he had been traveling around, doing music videos, appearing on TV, etc. He didn't want his female fans, ex-girlfriends, and side pieces to know he was with me. He didn't want me to see them all over him while he was portraying his image as a superstar single guy. This also went on for years.

I left my husband (who was my boyfriend at the time) and went back to New York. I wasn't feeling well and didn't know I was pregnant. I would have had two children by him, but I had an abortion. I wasn't ready to have a child because I had just had my son, Ahmante, a few years before my husband and I met. I'll never know if my husband resents me for that decision because he never spoke about it.

My husband helped me with my two older boys and did what he could when he had the money. He disciplined when he wanted to, whenever he was there. When I left for New York he didn't know I had gone. I just left. He didn't know where I was until I finally emailed him because a woman contacted me saying she was pregnant by him.

I still loved him and hoped that he loved me. He said he loved me and promised to take care of my children and I. He begged me to return to South Carolina. He even went to New York with a ring and asked me to marry him. I was pregnant, vulnerable, and confused. I knew I loved him, so I accepted his proposal. We were engaged for three years before we got married.

We didn't really get a chance to live in the house I bought in South Carolina happily because my husband was always at a club or out of town for "work." In fact, he was cheating on me with different women. He would always get caught, then lie about it. I don't think he has ever told me the truth, except for when he was drunk and yelling. That's when his real true feelings came out. The crazy part is that he felt no remorse for the things he said or did. He didn't try to apologize or even make up for his behavior.

Our whole marriage relationship was a total mess. It was so dysfunctional that I don't know how I survived being in it for so many years. In the back of my mind I held out hope that he was going to change. If I only I had been smart and strong enough then to get out or see the signs sooner.

I wanted to make our relationship work. I wanted to be married and live the dream. I wanted the house, husband, kids, and cars. We had all those things, but we weren't happy. We didn't have peace because we both treated each other unfairly. As a woman, I figured that getting married would change things between us because we would both feel more secure.

I was adamant about us getting married. In hindsight, I wish I had had someone to talk to about it because maybe I would have changed my mind about him. My husband wasn't much help because he went along with everything I said. I really thought we were both ready for this next step in our relationship. I was wrong.

I wanted to live right and raise my children in a good environment, not a hostile one. But my husband could not get it right. I wasn't perfect; I had my ugly, demanding ways. I only acted jealous because I loved him; I wanted his attention. I was never selfish with him. I gave that man everything I had and whatever he wanted. I cooked, cleaned, bought him cars and motorcycles, and bought him thousand of dollars worth of jewelry. I bought him clothes, burned them, then bought him some more.

Once he saw that I was no longer taking care of him, he began to treat me right.

It was too late because my attitude towards him slowly began to change. I started seeing him more and more as the manipulator he was. He claimed to never have any money and didn't put any effort into buying gifts or making things special for me. I gave up on him being a provider. When it came time to pay the bills and other things, I just went ahead and took care of everything.

I picked up the slack where he failed because he constantly said he was busy and had things to do. I was the one who worked. He only worked at night, on some days of the month, or on weekends. Somehow he was gone early in the morning every day. Sometimes I had to make an appointment for sex or set a date for us to go out. He never had time to go on vacations. When he did have time for a date, he would fall asleep in the car or be on his phone. We didn't talk, laugh, or anything on the way to the restaurant or movies, so I eventually just stopped going out with him. He would ask me to go out and I would turn him down because I already knew the date was going to be boring.

As long as we were out drinking and partying, he was good. But that is not the life I wanted to live because he couldn't be happy about anything in his life, even when we were out having a good time. I've said this before: I tried to make him happy by doing things that only pleased him, even if I was miserable.

There was no romance; it just seemed as if I was the one making the effort to keep the relationship going. I put all the work into my marriage. I introduced him to God, the church, and baptism. I asked that we get counseling to help resolve some of our issues. We attended one session but never went back because he didn't want to pay $150 each time. Even after the first session, he made it seem like he was going to change. Change came, but it wasn't for the better. I didn't change either. I believe that we both gave up on our marriage at that point.

It's never too late to speak up about what you're going through. You are not alone. I hid myself from the world and had bad mood swings. I couldn't think straight because my thoughts were cloudy. I was always in pain and alone in my bed. My boys tried to keep me company, but it was not like having my husband around to talk to.

Things had gotten so bad that my husband and I really couldn't even be in each other's presence. I nagged him just so he could leave the house. It was like we loved each other on some days and hated the sight of one another on other days. I think the love faded away even before we got married.

My children and I lived in secrecy. I didn't want anyone to know what I was going through behind closed doors. When I was out with him, I acted like we were so in love. I was his ride or die. He was my husband, so I wanted everyone who didn't like me to not like me even more because I was the hottest thing smoking because he married me.

When I went to the club, I made sure I looked my best by wearing fur coats, expensive clothes no one had or could afford, and high heels. My hair and nails were always on point. I did that because he made me feel like had to compete with other women who wanted him and didn't want to see him with me.

I used to take pills just to drown out the pain and heartache. I was so lost living in South Carolina without family or real friends. My husband kept me isolated for many years until I just started going out by myself to clubs. After some time, he began smearing my name in the streets, saying that I was crazy, jealous, and mean. No one wanted to get to know me because of that. Maybe I was all those things because of the way he treated me. I moved my entire life down to South Carolina for him, and he had the nerve to mistreat me. All I ever wanted was for him to love me the way I loved him.

Living with depression, I didn't know what to do. I took my pain out on anyone who was close to me. My children didn't know when I was going to snap. I wanted to commit suicide several times throughout those years. I was angry and frustrated about my life. I hated everything about my husband. He was cheap, unsupportive, a liar, and a cheater. His mouth disgusted me.

The angrier I got, the more my head and stomach hurt. I was so tense that I couldn't even eat or sleep. I just wanted to die. I needed to get some help, so I saw a therapist and was put on antidepressants because I felt like I was going to lose my mind.

Don't lose yourself in your relationship. Be honest with yourself about your feelings and how you want to be treated. If you are in an abusive relationship of any kind, get help. Tell someone. You don't have to tell your friends, but tell someone you know who is going to help you get out of the situation. I didn't have any help. I told my friends, but no one was able to help me.

God moved me out of the relationship. When I was finally away from my husband, I could breathe. I have moved on and now my health is better. My mind is clear, so I can focus on my life, career, and future with my children and grandchild.

Chapter 7

CLIMBING THE MOUNTAIN

My children and I were ready for what came next in our lives. In 2018, I did not want to be at home doing nothing for my birthday, so I decided to plan a trip for the boys and I. I had been following a very powerful pastor who was having local book signing at the time, so I planned our trip around that.

Because of my health issues, I started taking a new approach to life. I did things as though they were an adventure and crossed items off my bucket list. I started building better memories with my boys. I know they will never forget that I was mean to them, cursed at them, and make them feel as low as I did, but I wasn't going to stop trying to repair what I had broken.

We decided to visit Charlotte, North Carolina on Labor Day weekend. I knew that the city was going to be lively. This was going to be a good getaway for the kids and I because I hadn't been able to do much with them for a few years after my health began taking a toll on me. The stress of being sick and tired of being sick and tired made me fed up with my marriage and living situation.

We got to Charlotte, checked into our hotel, and settled in. The first thing my 15-year-old son wanted was to go exploring and see what he could get into. He was a typical teenager. If you have one, you know how they are. He went to the pool to see if he could meet some young ladies because, of course, he thought he was a mack daddy at such a young age. My younger son and I stayed in the room relaxing, talking, and laughing. We were finally spending quality time together, and it was peaceful. I didn't feel any stress, so I was able to laugh and unwind.

Our first night there was Friday, but we didn't do much because I wanted to be fresh and ready for the next day. I had planned to attend the book signing and other events surrounding that. On Saturday morning, I was ready to take on the day. The book signing started at 12 noon at the Sheraton Hotel. When we arrived, we saw people from all over the world. It was a beautiful thing to see so many women show up to support this pastor.

We got inside and found a place to sit and wait for the festivities to begin. I remember a time when there was so much going on at the house that the boys didn't even spend time together; none of us did. I was determined to make this trip different. During lunch, we ordered food and sat at the bar. I had a Caesar salad, and the boys had buffalo wings. Just us spending that time away from all the craziness that was going on at home felt so good.

When the pastor entered the room, we started off with a prayer and held hands all across the room. I had no idea that the woman sitting next to me was going to become a long time friend. Now, two years later, we still speak and are part of each other's lives.

Attending the book signing was the day that I believe was the beginning of my change process. The pastor did not know me or my story, but we were able to get one-on-one time with her as she signed our books. When it was my turn to meet her, she looked at me and said she wanted me to go home and forgive. I busted out in tears.

I asked myself how she knew I was holding on to unforgiveness toward my husband. She said, "Once you do that [forgive], doors will begin to open up for you, and your life will never be the same."

Then, she looked at my son and asked me about him. I told her his name. Then she said to him, "Let me tell you something. You have a good mom, and I can tell she takes very good care of you. I want you to go home and write down everything you want to be in your life. I sense that you have ideas of becoming something great, and I want you to focus on becoming those things." I mean, she was on point with everything she said to us because that is exactly what we had been trying to do. That day was a game changer for all of us. I felt encouraged and inspired to move forward and never look back. I was ready to forgive and move on.

The next two days were smooth sailing. We went out to eat, shopped, and had a great time. We visited Carowinds, the amusement park, for the first time. Just when I didn't think things could be better, they did. I had to set the pace for what I wanted to happen in our lives. It was the best birthday I had had in a long time.

If I told you that you could experience the same thing I did, would you believe me? Well, you can! Like I said before, you set the pace in your life for the positive things that you want to happen. If I had never taken that trip, I would not have known what this next move of God was for my life.

Early Tuesday morning, we got ready to leave our hotel after an amazing weekend. We were ready to drive back home. I felt refreshed and energetic because I knew I had an assignment to finish when I got home. It was time to forgive and move on. I didn't necessarily have to stay in the relationship, but I had to forgive my husband for hurting me all those years and not stepping up to take care of my sons and I.

I had a journey ahead of me because the whole time driving home I thought about what I wanted to say and how I was going to say it. There was no good form of communication between my husband and I. I had nothing nice to say to him and didn't care to speak at all. If I never saw him again, I would be fine. But I knew that would be impossible because we had a son together.

The boys and I got home pretty late, so we went straight to sleep. I didn't get a chance to sit my husband down and say anything the first few days after I got back because our paths didn't cross for some reason.

I had to do something, though, because a hurricane was headed our way. I remember watching the news while I was at dialysis. Immediately I thought to myself, *God what am I going to do? I don't want to be in the same house with this man if there is a storm coming and the lights go out and we have to pull together to make sure the boys are ok.* By the time I got home and turned on the TV, the hurricane had become a category 4 storm. I had to make a choice and quickly, was i going to stay and ride the storm out or was i going to stay in that house with him. My decision came quickly i told the boys let's pack up and get out while we still had time. At this point I already had booked the hotel as we were packing. I have never been to Smyrna, Georgia before this evacuation but i didn't care as long as I didn't have to be around my husband. I can say that the storm came and swept me away with it, because as long as hurricane florence was in South Carolina i had no reason to go back. I saw this as my opportunity to stay in Georgia and start my life over. This was my new Beginning.

PART THREE:

SPIRITUAL, MENTAL, AND PHYSICAL HEALTH

Chapter 8

ANXIETY

I was always in a rush to do something because I thought it was going to cause a problem if I took too long. I used to get accused of all kinds of things. Because of my anxiety, I always wanted to just hurry up and do what I had to do to get back home. I didn't know that my husband had purposely left his iPad in my car so that he could track me when I left home.

One night, I went to see my male friend. We sat in my car talking, then my husband showed up jumped out the car and began to punch me in the face and ribs. He bruised my back where my kidneys are; I was on dialysis at that time. He beat me up so badly that I couldn't even move.

I didn't go home that night. Instead, I went and stayed at a hotel for a week. Because I didn't know he had been tracking me, he knew where I was staying and went banging on my hotel door. When that happened, I realized he had been tracking me.

I don't know how I was able to go back home, but I did. After I went to see the doctor and showed them what he had done to me, they were concerned that I was in danger. They wanted me to report him, but I didn't. I went home and acted like nothing ever happened.

Why did I return? Why didn't I report him? I was stupid and blind. But you don't have to be that way. You can get out.

You can see the signs if he is not treating you right or if she isn't treating you like you should be treated as a man. Leave before you make the same mistakes I did. Take your time and don't rush into things with someone you hardly know.

I was always scared, but the with the glory of God and the heavens opening up for me as I prayed, I received a word from God one morning. He said, "I am the truth and the light. Through praying and fasting you will see the vision I have for you." I thank God for his unchanging hands and his will in my life.

Only God can give you the fruit you need. In his peace you will find refuge, love, joy, strength, and comfort. Fear will keep you in a dark place, but the Lord can and will open doors for you. He opened my eyes wider. All I had to do was reach out and ask for help; he answered me. My God is better than anything on this earth.

I found a better way to deal with fear and began to reevaluate my life. I had a lot of time to pray and came out a different person with more positive views about my life. If my husband was unwilling to give me what I was willing to give him, it was time for me to remove him from life. I had spent too much time being good to him when he wasn't good to me. God helped me trust the process. With everything I had been through, I was able to gather enough strength to leave. You can do it, too. Just take one step, change your mindset, and let go of fear and anxiety.

Chapter 9

POSITIVE AFFIRMATIONS

I had to start loving myself in order to see my life clearly, the way God saw my life. God himself changed my life around. And I began to feel conformed to my new lifestyle. The old me had passed away, and the new me had been born again. I fully committed my life to Jesus. I surrendered everything to him. I spoke those things in my life that I wanted to change and that I needed to see happen in my life in order for me to deal with my relationships. I had to tell myself to get up every day and keep living.

You can do the same. Speak those things as though they were already happening in your life for you. Walk in your purpose. Talk like you know that you're a king or a queen.

There were days when I couldn't get out of bed, I just didn't feel like getting in the shower or combing my hair. I didn't even eat. Suddenly, a message appeared on the TV or a phone call came from someone who hadn't heard from or seen me in a while. They had no clue what was going on with me. Even though I was in a slump, God always found a way to bring me out of it. Believing the words of the Bible is good for the soul.

When you think you're stuck or in trouble, know that God is working things out. Just be patient and hold on. I heard the Lord tell me to stop saying "I can't win for losing" because I defeated myself when I did. All this time I had been blocking my own blessings by standing in my own way with anger, bitterness, and holding onto the horrible things my husband said to me. I thought hurting him the way he destroyed me was a good way to make him feel the same pain I did.

I wasn't innocent either. I did some horrible things as well, and there was no justification for it. I won't make excuses for myself, but I was not the one bringing the strife into our home and marriage.

Once I began letting all of that go, I started speaking positive things into my life. I told myself: *I am worthy. I am beautiful. I am loved. I am a child of God. I am blessed.* My life started to change. I felt stronger. I felt powerful. I knew God had heard my prayers and answered me.

God began taking me down the path of righteousness. This was the beginning of my recovery. Recovery is a process of sustaining a whole, healed, and healthy life. The outcome of the process is the journey to prayer and repentance!

Chapter 10

PRAYING AND READING THE BIBLE

I prayed every day, even if it was a bad day, in order to build myself up. I did it to release myself from the bitterness and anger I had felt every day I spent in that house. I had to pray. I had to go back to church. I had to stop sleeping on God.

I couldn't take it anymore. I told God something had to give. My life wasn't where it was supposed to be; it wasn't where I wanted it to be. I wanted out of my marriage so badly that I daydreamed about a better life in a better place. I needed to be connected to God. Even though I was praying, I needed more people to pray for me.

It was easier for me to handle what God had coming my way. It was easier for me to see what was in store for me, so it was imperative that I didn't give up. Do some soul searching for your heart and mind to be cleansed of all the toxic things you were told by your abuser. I found that eliminating one thing at a time really helped me get past the hurt and pain.

I had taken the time to get to know myself. If you have never been to the beach alone, I suggest you take a day and go. It is calming and relaxing. I did nothing but lay in the sun, eat food, drink water, finish a puzzle, read my Bible, and take selfies. I met some new people, which was a great thing because we had good conversations.

Sometimes you have to step out of your comfort zone and do things that are unlike you. You will be amazed at the feeling you get. The thing you learn about yourself is that you don't always need a crowd. Once I started seeing things clearly, I was able to let some people go who said they were my friends. In actuality, their loyalty was to my husband, not me.

One of the difficult things I had to do was say goodbye to some people because they were not going to help me move forward to a more positive, productive version of myself. The people who came into your life when you were being abused have to go because they will only keep you down and remind you of all the pain you endured in the past. Some of them were only present because they wanted to be nosy and hear how my relationship wasn't working; they didn't care about me. I finally figured that out and started pruning those thorns.

I cut people off without warning! I didn't owe them any explanations. Why? Well for starters, if you are in the same place doing the exact same thing as when we met, this means you serve no purpose in my life. I only deal with people who show evidence of growth. Anything and anyone who will hinder your spiritual growth and life development has to be moved out of the way. End of story.

A good friend of mine said, "I stay away from those people who are everywhere but really nowhere." It is so true. I finally understood exactly what he meant because those are the people I cut off without warning. I felt no love was lost when I reevaluated my actions after the fact.

I had a lot of time to pray and evolve into a different person with a healthier view of my life. God told me that He had the final say. I was entering the best days of my life. God said, "Who told me that this was the end? Who told you that you were going to be on dialysis for the rest of your life?" He told me my life was just beginning. If I gave up, I wouldn't see what God had in store for me.

Chapter 11

MEDITATE

As I began to love myself, my relationship with everyone changed. I really hated when people tried to take advantage, manipulate a situation, drain you of your energy, or swindle you out of money so they could stay above water. People like that come out losing all the time. No one has the right to dump on you because their life isn't going the way they want it to. Don't let anyone transfer their negative spirit to you. Your mind has to be strong so that bad words cannot manipulate your feelings and how you view yourself. There is a real God who tells you that nothing and no one can or will make you believe anything other than what he says about you.

Carry on and make your life better. Open your mind and heart. Elevate yourself and your mind. Scripture says, "When you walk with wise people, you will be wise" Proverbs 13:20 (ASV). It's true in the positive and negative sense. Proverbs 11:13 says, "If you hang around a gossip, you'll become a gossip" (ASV). Think about it this way: for every peace stealer you let in your life, you are twenty percent more likely to live upset, be sour, and have a crisis. I'm asking you to find some positive people.

When you talk the talk, you gotta walk the walk because it pays the cost to be the boss. It doesn't take money to be real with yourself or anyone else. If someone doesn't agree with your actions to try to elevate yourself, then that means you're moving forward towards your goals. Those people are just not on your level. Your goal in life may not be theirs.

I could find a million things to complain about every day. But why should I? I am alive. Even though I go through so much in my life, I don't want to find any wrong. I meditate during my prayer time because my mind would run crazy otherwise. I had to try something because in my house was turmoil and strife. My kids fought each other because that is what they heard and saw.

Through meditation, I was able to regain my mental health and build my strength. I prayed, fasted, and asked God to help me heal. God is awesome; he reigns over my life. And he can do the same for you. I live for me, so you live for you. No one has the right to mistreat you. I won't believe anything else anyone says about me. I won't trust anyone who is not speaking positivity into my life. I want you to believe the same thing for yourself.

Chapter 12

TAKE A WALK OR GO FOR A DRIVE

I was in the hospital when God spoke to me. I let him lead the way in making a decision that had been weighing me down. I prayed, and he answered. He told me not to fight anymore. He told me to let him fight for me. He said, "You just sit back. Move out the way. I got you!" That night, I did just that. I laid my burden down.

God can and will fight your battles. You can cast your burdens upon the Lord, and he will carry you through. It took some time for me to apply the word of God to my life. But I decided that if I wanted a change, I had to go full force and be completely committed to God. There was no turning back for me because God had saved me and brought me out of the wilderness.

There were times when I didn't have an answer to any of the problems I was facing. After being abused in so many ways that broke me to pieces, I would stand up, get dressed, and leave the house. I would go for a drive or walk around the mall; sometimes retail therapy was my relief because spending money made me feel better.

In my experience, I was okay with who I was in an abusive relationship because I looked for ways to make myself feel better.

I thought it was a form of healing, but I was just masking my pain so that no one would notice how bad I was hurting.

You deserve to live a life free of strife and transgressions, but only you can make that choice for yourself. Believe me, very few people will take you by the hand and help you. The only one I know who will do that is God. You have to want freedom so badly that you cry out to Jesus to help you out of your circumstances.

Watching my mother get into fist fights with her boyfriends was normal to me. Being physically, mentally, verbally, and emotionally abused wasn't a display of real love. What I experienced was manipulation and downright disgraceful. When my husband raised his hand to hit me, it wasn't because I was mouthing off to him. He did it because that was his way of controlling me. It wasn't a sign of strength. It was him showing how weak he was.

Some men and women hurt other people because they have been hurt before. They never took the time to understand why they had to experience pain. In the beginning, I didn't understand why my brother molested me. I didn't get why my mother hurt me the way she did. Everything makes sense now. She was hurt by her mother. No one taught my brother that he wasn't supposed to touch me (or any girl) like that.

Many people said I looked happy and that it didn't look like I was being abused, but they didn't live in my house. They didn't know the person that was hurting me like I knew him. When you feel overwhelmed by what is going on in your life, find an outlet or place where you can go and feel free to be yourself.

Chapter 13

LISTENING TO POSITIVE MUSIC

There were many days when I was lost in confusion and hurt, but I always found some solace in listening to music. I listened to whatever made me feel better in the moment, songs that were uplifting and encouraging. Some made me cry or replay the chain of events that took place, but they got me through the hard times.

One year, I had gotten into a fight with my husband around Thanksgiving. I mean, it was a drag out fist fight over infidelity. I could not get out of bed, but I knew that I had to prepare some food. I had a king-size bed that was high off the floor, so I had to literally climb out of bed. I dangled my feet off the bed first, then I sat up. I took a few deep breaths and released the tension from my neck and shoulders. I was in a lot of pain.

After I finally got up, I went to the bathroom, turned on the shower, and let the water run for a bit to get it nice and hot. I reached over for my iPod, and the first thing that came on was a gospel song. I let it play as I sat under the water, drowning myself in the song. I put my whole head under the water so that the soreness of my face and head would stop throbbing. All I could hear under the water were the lyrics "hold on, change is coming."

Once I finished showering, I continued listening to music because my spirit was uplifted. Gospel music made me feel better because the songs were uplifting and encouraging. When you had nothing but toxic thoughts every day, like I did, it feels good to hear something positive. I felt powerful listening to certain songs that played.

It may not seem like the music you listen to makes a difference in your life, but it does. If you listen to positive, uplifting songs enough, you will start to believe what you're hearing. I know listening to the lyrics of almost any gospel song will make me cry. Once I released my emotions, I was able to go on another day. Honestly, I believe that is how I was able to get through a lot of my lonely nights.

Find one song or an entire playlist of tracks that will help you through your situation. Don't let another day, bruise, or bump stop you from enjoying what makes you happy. I didn't have any sense of feeling for anything on dark, gloomy days after a night of arguing or an afternoon of non-stop fighting. I exhausted myself having to always defend my words or actions. I couldn't concentrate, let alone listen to music. Somehow, by the divine grace of God, a song always came on the TV or radio as I drove that spoke directly to my situation or exact emotion at the time.

Even when you don't think that a song matters or could help you, it can. I realized that I loved music, and it brought me great joy. I found a part of myself in music, and you can as well. Even if you have to make up your own song and sing out loud to get you through your pain, do it. There is always a way out of every situation you find yourself in.

Chapter 14

CONGRATULATE YOURSELF

Each time I left an abusive relationship, looking back at those times and reflecting on it, I never got past any of the hurt. I only landed in another abusive relationship; each one was a different kind of abuse. That is, until I met my husband; our relationship lasted for over 17 years. This was the one that almost took me to my deathbed. But after getting out, with the help of my Lord and Savior and my children, I found it to be so much easier on my health and state of mind.

Leaving a spouse or significant other who is hurting you is a huge move forward in your life, so you have to congratulate yourself for even taking the very first step to your recovery. On some days, you will feel angry at yourself for being tricked into an abusive relationship, and you will feel trapped. But you have to learn to forgive yourself. It was not your fault the person you were with treated you badly.

Being emotionally abused leaves scars that no one can see. It was up to me to try and heal myself for the sake of my health and my children. No one should be abusive to anyone. I shouldn't have had to go through pain for so many years, especially when I trusted this person with my life and the lives of my children. Through it all, I kept on going and fighting with every inch of my being. I knew one day I was going to get out; I just didn't know how.

On the day when I finally left my husband, I felt such relief. I decided to go to Atlanta, Georgia on September 11, 2018. Hurricane Florence had quickly approached the South Carolina coast. My oldest boys and I set out for Georgia; my youngest stayed with his dad. I suspect my husband made him stay. I guess my husband had the idea that I was not coming back, so he didn't want me to take him. Maybe he thought he wasn't ever going to see his son again. The only reason he did that was because he knew I was financially stable.

I chose to go to Smyrna, and we stayed there for two weeks. The day that we were supposed to go back home, my son, Tarel, asked if we could stay in Georgia and buy a house. I asked him if he was sure. He said that he didn't feel stressed in Georgia and didn't want to go back to South Carolina. I thought it would have been a great idea for us to move.

I had been looking for a place to live in South Carolina, but I never got approved. We began the search for houses in Smyrna and found a couple of realtors who were showing houses while we were there. We saw three houses the first day, but we didn't like them. The second day we saw two houses, but we didn't like those either. On the third day, after viewing six houses, we saw one we had prayed for; that is the house I live in now.

My son had asked me a while back if I could find a two-story house, so we fell in love when we walked into this house.

The owner was welcoming. She listened to our story about being evacuees; we just wanted a new life and a fresh start. She talked to my son and listened to what he had to say. I think she liked what she heard because, at the end of it all, she told us she trusted us and would give us a chance.

If I tell you that the next day I signed my lease and had the keys in my hand, you wouldn't believe me. Yes, I signed the lease to my new home in Atlanta and was preparing to relocate. This move was not planned; it just happened.

The thing about it is that I know that it was a move of God because I had tried to apply for houses in South Carolina but could not get approved. This time around, it felt different and went smoothly. The landlord did not give me a hard time about anything. From that moment forward, I knew that it was meant to be. I prayed even harder because I was thankful that God opened that door for us to freedom.

The best part of this is that I recognized the doors that were closed on me as God doing his thing to move me where he wanted me. You know that when one door closes another door opens, right? That is what began happening when we decided to stay in Georgia.

We stayed in Georgia for another two weeks. The boys didn't go to school during that time. We bought blow-up mattresses, a TV, sheets, pillows, and food. I called to have the utilities turned on in my name on October 1, 2018. That was our official move-in date.

All I had to do was go back, pack up my house, and have a moving company transport everything to Georgia. And that is what I did. When I got to South Carolina on the 28th of September, the boys and I began packing. It took us three days to pack up our four-bedroom house. We were happy it was time to go; we knew that nothing was going to stop us because we had the keys to our new lives.

Chapter 15

RECONSTRUCTION

Forgiving your abuser isn't for the perpetrator; it's for you. When you forgive, you're letting him or her know you are in control. I reminded myself that in order to release and move on, I had to say something. I sent my husband a text message. I didn't actually tell him that I forgave him, but it was something to that extent. I let him know that I was no longer going to be an angry individual and that I was done with all the mess and going back and forth. In his mind, he thought I was letting it all go and our marriage was still in tact That was not what I meant. After pushing me away, not mending things when they were broken, and still doing the same thing, I got tired of being stepped on and manipulated.

Narcissists like to keep you as their victim and in a perpetual state of fear, control, and manipulation. Because there was such long-term verbal abuse on both our parts, I broke down emotionally and mentally. I was completely unsure of myself. I was unable to recognize my true value and didn't trust anything my husband said anymore.

Forgiveness is a ten-letter word that has so much power. What was I forgiving my husband for? I was freeing him from bondage. I was sure that if I asked God to forgive me of my sins that God would grant me that forgiveness. Forgiveness allows release from unseen bondage and requires the granting of grace and mercy. Free the person who has hurt you, just like God has freed you.

"Bless Jehovah, o my soul; and all that is within me; bless his holy name. Bless Jehovah, o my soul, and forget not all his benefits: who forgiveth all thine iniquities;who redeemeth thy life from destruction" (Psalm 103 ASV).

"Forbearing one another, and forgiving each other, if any man have a complaint against any; even as the Lord forgave you, so also do ye" (Colossians 3:13 ASV).

It took me a long time to forgive. I always thought about how it felt to just let go and not be hurt anymore. After a lot of soul searching, I realized that forgiveness isn't about accepting or excusing my abuser's behavior. Forgiveness is about letting go and preventing his behavior from ever destroying my heart again.

Do you want the keys to your new life? You know what I did to get it. You, too, can begin to shift your life by making the decision that you want better for yourself and your children (if you have any). Your kids deserve to be in a happy, healthy environment. If you're in an unhealthy relationship, such as the one I was in, you have to make that move for you and your children.

You can use these strategies:
1. Determine that you are going to leave.
2. Decide where you want to go.
3. Make sure you plan to leave when it's safe.
4. Remind yourself that God will see you through.

5. Execute your plan.

Now, if you're not financially stable and do not have the means to move or get out, look into temporarily living in shelters. If your situation is where you have to leave overnight, you can call Safe Horizon for help. I know this from experience. They will not disclose your location to anyone, so you have to be willing and ready to make this life altering decision for your safety.

I am finally free from the physical abuse; that was step one of my freedom. I decided to focus on things that I never had time for before. Think of creative things you can do with your life. I had to figure out a way to channel my energy in other positive ways because I was mad as hell and wanted to get back at my husband for everything he put me through. Once I moved out and began to look for other outlets for releasing my emotions, it gave me something else to think about.

When I moved out, I had already had my business up and running. I decided to throw myself into work and focused on starting a new life. I enjoyed the peace and quiet. I woke up early in the morning at about 5 am, said my morning prayer, had a cup of tea, and began my day. I went on my porch and watched the sunrise. It was calming and peaceful; that's all I ever wanted after all I had been through.

This newfound freedom was liberating. I remember some days when I went outside, drove to the mall, or just searched for something to eat. It's like my appetite picked up a whole lot more. I was beginning to be my happy self. Finding myself was hard because my identity was never who I was; it was always about being someone's wife. I was never addressed by name, so my identity was gone. Once you begin to discover who you are on your own, things that you thought of yourself will no longer be the same.

I learned to play Bingo. I know that might sound a little crazy because you may have this image of old people in a hall playing the game, but it was actually helpful because I did something with my time. I went to play Bingo five days a week, Thursday through Monday. I even went on my dialysis days. I didn't care if I was tired afterwards; it kept me away from having to look at my husband or hear his voice because everything about him bothered me. This was something for me. And I had fun doing it.

Don't run away from the problems like I did. Run from the abuse. Don't let anyone ever put you down or make you feel uncomfortable in your own house, especially if you have children in the home.

PART FOUR:

FORGIVE YOURSELF

Chapter 16

AVOID CONTACT WITH YOUR ABUSER

I was so done with the chapter of abuse in my life that I cut off all communication with my husband because he was a narcissist. The accusations and torment he put me through were horrible. I used to get accused of all kinds of things like having oral sex in a parking lot. I got accused of being seen coming out of a hotel with one of my customers from my old business. It was crazy because, at that same time, my husband and I were together out on a date.

He constantly called me names. I mean, who wants to be woken up out of their sleep to be accused of being at a hotel? I had no idea what he was talking about, but the people he listened to were helping him create these images in his head and encouraging him to beat me down verbally. He was dumb enough to listen, so I realized that I had to change this.

Even though we were still living together, I completely stopped texting and calling him for anything. I had to depend on my children for everything. That was not the best thing to do because now the responsibility was on my oldest son to take care of his brothers and me. I was able to get up and go as freely as I wanted to, without getting accused of cheating. The words didn't stop, just the accusations did. It actually got worse with the verbal abuse.

I had a conversation with a friend of mine who was in a marriage that just wasn't working out. It was never physically abusive, but it wasn't a happy one. She shared with me that her ex thought that she wouldn't be able to make it without him. In his head, she would always need him. That is mental abuse because he felt that as long as he had control over her mind, body, and finances that she wouldn't be able to do without him. In many ways but one he wanted control over her, so she made up her mind that she wasn't going to let him take over her life by using money to get what he wanted or as a leash to hold on to her. She set herself free when she made the choice to say no.

When you feel that enough is enough and begin to see past the hurt and pain, you can begin to take back your life with a simple "no." Stand on those same words. No means no and enough is enough.

Chapter 17

GET SOME REST

I went for days without sleeping; I had insomnia. It seemed like I couldn't sleep at night, but I always wanted to sleep during the day. I remember waking up early in the morning and wanting to go back to sleep.

I needed to rest because I was tired of being sick and tired. Lack of sleep leads to stress, anxiety, not healing. Take some time for yourself during and after a traumatic breakup. If you don't, things can start to spiral downward in your healing process. You will likely begin to feel exhausted, if you don't already. Sleep as late as you want or need to without any worries about anyone but yourself. If you have a job that allows you to move your schedule around, change your shift to make sure you're getting enough sleep.

During this process of getting rest make sure you are taking care of your body. Recovering from any kind of abuse can take a toll on your body. Physical abuse is the most painful thing to experience, so with that make sure you heal yourself properly and let your mind body and soul rest.

Chapter 18

EXORCISE THE ABUSIVE COMMENTS

"I will not have a pity party with anyone who wants to wallow in their own mess. Get up and do something about it. What are you waiting for? There is no pain in the world that is going to stop me from getting to my destiny." That is what I wrote down every day as I thought about what I was being told about myself by my husband. *I was no good. I was dirty. I was a smut. I was a whore. No one is going to love me because I was mean. I was bitter. I was a drama queen.* I was being degraded with words. The best thing for me was to write down all he said. It wasn't so that I could remember the things that I was told about myself, but it was for me to remember that I was not any of those words or things he said I was.

I want you to write down the criticisms that haunt you and cause you to undervalue yourself. Then, let them go. Don't try to reason with, refute, or even disagree with the criticism. The ones saying those things are not worthy of that. Tear it up. Flush it down the toilet. Hell, have a bonfire. Destroy those negative comments as a ritual.

Let your abuser go and never think of him or her again. After you have left your abuser, don't look back. You could call him or her up and curse them out. But ask yourself why you would waste your energy on holding on to the bad things they said about you. It is very important that you don't remember these comments that were made. Do not obsess over the negativity or the content of the emotional abuse that you endured.

Don't argue with the criticism or with the abuser. Don't refute the criticism because it wasn't worth listening to from the beginning. It is beneath you now. You may feel that you were abused because you were not worthy, interesting, or attractive enough. All that is not true. You were abused because someone cruel chose to mistreat you. At this stage in your life, when you find yourself feeling down about the false messages your abuser spoke over you, use your list of positive memories to remind yourself that you have lots of good qualities. You make the choices in your life, no one else.

PART FIVE:

SPIRITUAL BELIEFS THAT GIVE MEANING TO YOUR LIFE

Chapter 19

BE PATIENT WITH YOURSELF

While married, I had so much hate in me that I didn't know how to get rid of it. I wanted to be happy and at peace with myself about everything that had happened, but I wasn't being patient with myself. Living in that house was a nightmare. I mean, I just couldn't stand the sight of that man. I was always told that I played the victim and never took responsibility for my actions. I know that I wasn't perfect in our relationship, but that doesn't justify the beating he gave me every time he thought he could. Abusers don't think that they are damaging your sense of self-respect or your self image because they can't see anything but themselves.

The healing process takes time. Don't rush trying to suppress the abuse and the damage that has been done to you. Be gentle with yourself, your thoughts, and how you move past this stage.

It is not an easy journey; I know it wasn't for me. I still believe that I need more time because I can't expect everything to happen all at once. It is going to take some time to rebuild and repair the damage from the abuse.

Take some time off from work, school, or whatever responsibilities you have to clear your head. How long? A week? A month? Who knows! You can only move through your process at your own pace.

I know for me it was getting out of that house and running away from it all that helped. There was no communication. As long as I didn't have to hear or see him, it was like a weight had been lifted off of me. I needed to be patient with myself because I was so far gone.

I would rather not tell you get over it, but I will tell you that avoiding your emotions will not help the process. Take your time. You may process things quicker than others, or you may need help getting through it. After a breakup, you need to process your emotions by recognizing what you need, responding to those needs, and reflecting on your experience. When you do those three things and realize that processing and suppressing your emotions are two different issues, that is when you give yourself room to grow and heal.

Chapter 20

FORM NEW GOALS

I finally decided to go back to school and get my GED. I had waited so long for this opportunity. My mind was not in the right place all those years back when I tried in 2006. I had gotten pregnant with my last child, who is now 12 years old, and I didn't have it in me to go back.

Once I cleared my mind and got rid of all the clutter in my life, it was time to make some new goals in my life and get my diploma; that was just the beginning. Starting new goals in your life after you have experienced trauma and disappointments will help you. You can and will overcome the abuse. You are the champion of your own life. For me, I have become just that. Life throws curveballs at me, but it is how I deal with them that matters.

I love me. I said this to myself as I began to think of new things I could do in my life. *Today, you will not bring me down or upset my life. I refuse to let you steal my joy. I am changing my life and my thought process without you. I love me.* When you confess with your mouth what you want for your life, the abuser no longer has control. Set your goals and standards higher than before.

I am moving on. Doors are opening for me. All I had to do to get to this point was reach out and ask for help. Now, I am rising above the abuse and the negative criticism that was spoken over me. I am making new memories and setting new goals for my life. This is what I believe will help you. If you have a poor mouth, you will have a poor life.

Chapter 21

SPIRITUAL BELIEFS THAT GIVE MEANING TO YOUR LIFE

I've made huge mistakes and some very bad decisions. I wish I could turn back the hands of time so that I could live a normal life. I prayed and asked God to show me what I was doing wrong. I knew that there was a higher being that was in control of my life, but I did not know what my purpose for being in this relationship was. I read Scriptures that could help me because my spiritual beliefs are what kept me going. I knew that I had to stand for something, or I would continue to fall for whatever my husband brought to the table.

Every day that God gives me is a gift. When he stops giving it to me, that means I get to be with him. It was time for me to do right and live for God and my children. I decided to be obedient, kind, caring, and loving.

I set goals for myself at the beginning of 2019. I knew that my life was not going to be the same once God changed it. He will change yours, too. We will win!

This year will be a year that will bring me much success and wealth. In 2019, I will receive good health reports from the doctors and consistently eat better. Setting these goals for myself, I knew that I couldn't leave any more room for failure or disappointment. This year, write down what will happen for you and what you want to change.

(This should say focus points with lines so that the reader can write down their thoughts)

Chapter 22

JOIN A CHURCH

When I moved to Atlanta, I already knew New Mercies Christian Church was where I wanted to attend because I had gone there many times when I hung out in Georgia. I have grown so much since I have been part of this ministry. Believe in God to see you through your storm so that you can come out equipped with the strength you need to overcome this battle of abuse you have endured. The scars will still be there but, through God and his Word, you will be healed.

It was just the beginning when I first moved. I was happy, free, and could finally file for divorce. I was able to go to church and fellowship with other women who understood what I had gone through. My pastor is the truth; he brought the Word of God to life. The Holy Spirit was all over me.

Recovery is a process of sustaining a whole, healed, and healthy life. When I repented, God restored. You have to keep on fighting.

It's a war! Give your life to God and watch how he works in your favor. When joining a church, make sure your spirit is led to the right house of God. Let me tell you something: you are the church. Your body is the holy temple. In order for you to heal and overcome your abuse and your abuser, seek God's grace and mercy.

I am now a single mom and alone with these thoughts of how can I get myself together. Joining the church was a great start for me. Now, I attend Bible study every Wednesday and go to service each Sunday.

My life changed when I completely surrendered everything to God. I no longer did things my way. I started applying the Word of God to my daily life and changing the old things I used to do into the new way God wanted me to do things. In order for you to live out your dreams and goals in life to be able to see that you are worth far more than what your abuser said you were, you have to turn your life over to God. He is the only way, the truth, and the life.

Chapter 23

JOIN A SUPPORT GROUP

When you get away from your abuser and feel comfortable enough to go out, tell people what you have been going through. I suggest you join a support group. Talking to others and learning from other abuse survivors can be an important step in your recovery. Support groups form an environment for you to feel comfortable and safe for whatever you are about to say; it won't leave the room. They teach you the skills to cope and move on.

When you are ready to take back your life, find the nearest support group in your area. Don't be afraid because you are not alone. I have been there, just like there are many other men and women who have been in the same predicament. Don't feel ashamed to tell your story; it will help the healing process.

It was hard for me to be alone on some days. I sat in my room and thought about the things I could have been doing with the man that I loved so much. I even had thoughts of going back because it just all seemed so familiar. I think we all feel that way at first. It's natural for us to want companionship and love, especially during times of transitions.

Surround yourself with friends, animals, or a new experience. Do not respond to any offers from your abuser. Don't go back when you want companionship. Find it elsewhere. I can honestly say that I had no idea what I was doing once I left, but sharing about my tumultuous relationship with others helped me process the whirlwind of emotions.

Remember this: never be afraid to tell someone what is going on if you are being abused. You deserve to be treated with respect. Getting punched, kicked, or even slapped is not love. Don't let anyone tell you that you are not worthy of happiness, love, or peace of mind.

Chapter 24

SPEAK POSITIVE THINGS OVER YOUR LIFE

I had to learn to speak over my life and the things that I wanted to see happen. For many years, I just wasn't myself. I catered to everyone else's needs, except mine. I neglected myself because I felt worthless inside. I looked good on the outside and that made me want to change the way I saw myself. *I am a child of God. I am a Queen. I am more than a conqueror.*

Speak life into yourself. Tell yourself that you are worthy of love, peace, and joy. Tell yourself that you will no longer let another man or woman abuse you in any kind of way. Tell yourself that you can and will make it through the storm, as long as you have God on your side and know that he said you shall live and not die; you can and will live. I did it, and so can you!

Jesus set me free. When he set me free, I had to become fearless. I became a fearless witness. I had faith that God was going to do all the things he had promised. Jesus showed me the power of love. Once he began the healing process within me, I fell madly in love with him. My heart opened up and my mind was at ease. There was no more stress or late nights waking up in cold sweats. I no longer felt torment inside.

People deal with insecurities. I dealt with low self-esteem. I didn't feel pretty, sexy, or thick enough. There were areas of my body that I wish were fuller, but none of that mattered once I knew who I was in Christ. I felt comfortable in my own skin. God helped me to build walls that will keep me from ever going back to an abusive relationship. God can help you. Just give God a chance; he will see you through. I promise.

I became fearless and transparent. I learned not to fear my journey and to experience new things. God is the only one who can make a new path for me. Isaiah 43:19 (ASV) says, "Behold, I will do a new thing; now shall it spring forth; shall ye not know it?" I no longer had to fight my abuser with words or objects because it wasn't my battle.

Here's how you fight your battles and get back up:

1. Know your opponent.
2. Accept that the battle is already won.
3. Catch up to your faith.
4. Claim what's yours.

God has given us everything we need to survive. When I changed my attitude, my heart followed. Never allow another human being to keep you from the promises of Jesus Christ.

Chapter 25

RECOVERY

I once heard someone say that God releases you for his glory. This is not the season to impress anyone because I know who I am. I heard the Holy Spirit tell me that I was free. I was forgiven, so I forgave myself for the self-guilt. I forgave myself for the stupid decisions I made. I forgave myself for putting my children in the middle. I knew that all the things I did and said in all those years of verbal, mental, and physical abuse were wiped away.

I had to forgive the one man I gave my life to who did the most damage to me. It was time I faced the music to let go and let God. Someone once told me that I could not stay in something built for the dead. The doubt and guilt that I had inside from believing what I thought was real love from my relationship was removed by God.

We have joy, peace, and love because of the power of God. We have the recovery process because of the power of God. Recovery is the process of sustaining a wholeheartedly healthy life.

I am in recovery! The process of recovery is in connection with abuse and the road to mental recovery. Recovering from hurt, disappointment, physical, mental, and verbal abuse is a process that no one should face alone. Everyone needs compassion.

When you think of all the things you have been through and do some reflection, you will see that you will be able to admit your mistakes. If you're not moving, you're not prospering. God knows how to get you to refocus. Recovery requires me admitting my wrongs. I know I played a part in my relationships. Yes, I also called these men out their names and hit them. To me, I was defending myself. There is no justification for the abuse or the abuser.

My recovery involves giving God my past and accepting my future. I am happy with myself and know who I am in God. The spirit of recovery is that you have to have hope; your hope must be in God. Recovery is possible even at your worst time in life. God can work with something, even when there is nothing there. Recovery requires a proper connection to the people you know who want the best for you. They want the same things and have similar goals in life as you. Recovery gives birth to new life expectations. You will no longer live with someone else's expectations. The outcome of recovery is a process, not a journey.

The culmination of my journey while writing this book was reminiscent of childbirth; the contents of my book are delivered in love. Even with some scars as proof of where I have been, I will not let them keep me from going where I am headed in the future. So many times we want to say that we will be okay, but in reality we are scared individuals who strive to be better under the circumstances.

In my reality, what I went through and what you have read is not the end of my life; it is just the beginning. Sharing my story with the world certainly was a difficult decision because I had to realize who I was and who I have become. I decided to share with you all what the inside of my life looked like for many years.

I fought with everything I had. I learned how to live each day as if it were the most beautiful day, despite the abuse. At the end of the relationship, your mind and body still fight with you to reconstruct all the damage. It is a very long process, but I know that you can and will have a better future when you make that decision for yourself.

EVALUATING MY RELATIONSHIP

The purpose of this exercise is to help you start thinking about different aspects of your relationship. If you are not in a dating relationship right now, think about a past or present relationship with a friend or family member. Ask yourself the following questions about that person and your relationship with him or her.

I am evaluating my relationship with: _____

1. List five things about this person that you really like.

    _____

    _____

    _____

2. Write down five things about this person that you really dislike.

    _____

    _____

    _____

3. Do you think this person's relationships with family and friends are healthy? Why or why not?

_____

_____

_____

4. Does this person encourage you to have other friends or discourage other friendships? In what way?

_____

_____

_____

5. List three things that this person is interested in besides you.

_____

_____

_____

6. List three activities that you participate in without this person.

_____

_____

_____

7. Do you both have equal decision-making power in your relationship?

_____

_____

_____

8. How do the two of you usually handle conflict?

_____

_____

_____

9. Since you have been in this relationship, do you generally feel better or worse about yourself or about the same?

_____

_____

_____

FOCUS ON EMOTIONAL ABUSE

Emotional abuse is a way of hurting someone without necessarily being physical. It's when one person in a relationship tries to control the other person's feelings or thoughts in order to gain power over them.

I am evaluating my relationship with: _____

_____

I have done this to this person. This person has done this to me:

1. Put-down: calling names, telling them they're stupid or ugly, not good enough, or no one could ever love them
2. Frequently cursing or yelling at the other person
3. Threatening or making the other person feel nervous or scared
4. Frequently criticizing or correcting the other person (the way they look, talk, etc.)
5. Lying or cheating
6. Playing mind games or making the other person think they're crazy
7. Putting responsibility for your behavior on the other person
8. Making fun of or putting down the other person's family, culture, religion, race, or heritage
9. Embarrassing or humiliating the other person, especially in front of other people

Checkpoint - Circle one answer.

Am I being emotionally abused by my partner?

Yes No

Have I been emotionally abused in the past?

Yes No

Am I being emotionally abusive to my partner?

Yes No

Have I been emotionally abusive in the past?

Yes No

FOCUS ON PHYSICAL ABUSE

Physical abuse is any behavior that is meant to cause hurt to another person's body or to control another person's physical freedom or movement.

One person may abuse another using his or her own physical strength, an object or weapon, size, or presence to intimidate or control the other. Circle all that apply.

I am evaluating my relationship with: _____

Pushing or shoving

Grabbing

Hitting, slapping, or punching,

Pulling hair

Kicking

Choking

Holding down or grabbing their arm so they can't walk away

Throwing objects at him or her

Using weapons to hurt or threaten him or her

Biting, pinching, spitting

Arm twisting, burning

Carrying him or her without permission

Trapping him or her in a car

Abandoning him or her in an unsafe place

Chasing

Standing in the doorway to block him or her from leaving

Hiding car keys, shoes, clothes, or money so he or she can't leave

Standing in front of/behind the car to prevent him or her from leaving

Sabotaging a car to prevent him or her from leaving

Refusing to help him or her when sick or injured

Following or stalking

Check point:

Am I being abused by my partner?

Yes No

Have I been physically abused in the past?

Yes or No

Am I being abused physically abusive to my partner?

Yes No

Have I been physically abusive in the past?

Yes No

HOW HEALTHY IS MY RELATIONSHIP?

Below, list one of the healthy relationship characteristics and one unhealthy trait. Many relationships have a combination of both. The point of this exercise is to figure out what things in your relationship are healthy or unhealthy, so you can gain an appreciation for the best things and decide what you want to change. Read both lists and put a heart next to every statement that is true about your relationship.

I am evaluating my relationship with: _____

Is it healthy? _____

Put a check near the answer if you and this person...

Have fun together more often than not

Each enjoy spending time separately, with your own friends, as well as with each other's friends

Always feel safe with each other

Trust each other

Are faithful to each other, if you have made this commitment

Support each other's individual goals in life, like getting a job or going to college

Respect each other's opinions, even when they are different

Solve conflicts without putting each other down, cursing, or making threats

Both of you accept responsibility for your actions

Both of you apologize when you're wrong

Have equal decision-making power about what you do in your relationship

Both of you have control over your own money

Both of you are proud to be with each other

Encourage each other's interests, like sports or extracurricular activities

Have some privacy, your letters, diary, and personal phone calls are respected as your own

Have close friends & family who like the other person and are happy about your relationship

Never feel like you're being pressured for sex

Communicate about sex, if your relationship is sexual

Allow each other space, when needed

Always treat each other with respect

Is it Unhealthy? _____

Put a heart if you or this person...

Get extremely jealous or accuse the other of cheating

Put the other down by calling names, cursing or making the other feel bad about him or herself

Yell at and treat the other like a child

Don't listen when the other talks

Frequently criticize the other's friends or family

Pressure the other for sex, or make sex painful or feel humiliating

Have ever threatened to hurt the other or commit suicide if they leave

Cheat or threaten to cheat

Tell the other how to dress

Have ever grabbed, pushed, hit, or physically hurt the other

Blame the other for your own behavior ("If you hadn't made me mad, I wouldn't have...")

Embarrass or humiliate the other

Smash, throw, or destroy things

Try to keep the other from having a job or furthering his/her education

Make all the decisions about what the two of you do

Try to make the other feel crazy or plays mind games

Go back on promises

Act controlling or possessive, like you own your partner

Use alcohol or drugs as an excuse for hurtful behavior

Ignores or withholds affection as a way of punishing the other

Depends completely on the other to meet social or emotional needs

www.ingramcontent.com/pod-product-compliance
Lightning Source LLC
Chambersburg PA
CBHW021148090426
42740CB00008B/999